Bet you didn't know

7 feline facts to pounce on

1 A **tiger's** roar can be **heard** over one mile away.

2 **Cats** were domesticated at least **3,000 years** ago in Egypt.

3 ALL CATS ARE BORN WITH **BLUE EYES.**

4 Unlike most cats, **lions** are **excellent swimmers.**

5 Today's **domestic cats are cousins** of **big** cats.

6 A **tiger's paw prints** are called pug marks.

7 **Cats communicate** using at least 16 known **"cat words."**

Wolf Speak

Understanding the secret language of a wolf pack

Calling all pack members! Meet us over here **to go hunt!**

To all who can hear: If you're not in our pack, **stay off our turf.**

It's all good. **C'mon, let's go.**

I f you want to understand wolf speak, you need to use your ears, eyes, and even your nose. Wolves talk to each other using their voices, body language, and, yes, body odor.

Wolves live in packs. Their survival depends on working as a team to find food, protect pack members, and raise pups. Being able to clearly read and express each wolf's rank is a matter of great importance.

Read My Lips and Ears and Shoulders

From head to tail, wolves express information through subtle and obvious body language. Facial expressions and how high a tail is held tell a wolf's confidence level or where it fits within the pack. The higher a wolf ranks, the higher it stands and holds its head, ears, and tail. The lower it ranks, the lower it drops everything, even flopping to the ground belly side up. Wolves puff up their fur or flatten it to express themselves.

From Growl to Howl

Yips, yaps, barks, and squeaks are all wolf sounds. Wolves usually use vocals when interacting with each other. Scientists have trouble eavesdropping on these shy animals, so little is known about wolves' private conversations. But they're sure vocalizations are important. Even a three-week-old puppy can mimic almost all the adult sounds.

The howl is a wolf's long-distance call. In a forest, a howl might be heard six miles away. On the tundra it can be heard up to ten miles away. A wolf may howl to locate its pack. Or it may be announcing its availability to join or form a new pack. Packs howl together in a chorus to strengthen the team, warn other wolves away from their territory, or coordinate movements of pack members.

Talk to the Paw

With a sense of smell a hundred times better than humans', it's no wonder scent is an important part of wolf communication. Wolves intentionally leave their scent by marking trees and bushes with urine. They also secrete messages with scent glands in their feet and other body parts.

These odors aren't generally obvious to humans, but for wolves, sniffing tells all: the identity of an animal, its social status, whether it's an adult or a youth, how healthy it is, what it's been eating, if it's ready to breed, and much more.

As scientists keep learning how to understand wolf speak, they use their best tools—sniffing, spying, and eavesdropping.

GRAY WOLVES

You Are Here

CONTINENTS: EUROPE AND ASIA

COUNTRY: RUSSIA

SIZE: WORLD'S LARGEST COUNTRY, FOLLOWED BY CANADA, THE UNITED STATES, AND CHINA

LOCATION: NORTHWESTERN COUNTRYSIDE

Your plane lands in northern Russia. As you approach wolf territory, you hear them first. *Ow-oooo! Grrr!* Then you spot the pack of wolves. Wrestling and playing, they look like they're celebrating. They're actually psyching themselves up for a hunt. Wolves' preferred prey includes moose. One moose can weigh twice as much as the entire pack. Confidence and teamwork mean survival. Only about one in ten attacks on a moose is successful.

Packs are led by the dominant male and female, sometimes called the alpha wolves. Your heart pounds when you see the alpha female lunge toward a younger wolf in the pack. It falls down, exposing its neck to show submission. Growling, the alpha holds it down by its throat. Even from a distance, you understand the conversation. She's reminding the juvenile that she's in charge. The pup's submissive response means, "Yes, ma'am!" Communication and leadership help the pack survive.

You notice that the alpha pair really seem to like each other. The power couple nuzzles and cuddles; they're likely to remain lifelong partners. The two leaders rally the pack, and all but one adult trot off to hunt. Left behind: the pups and an adult babysitter. You watch as the wolves, working as a team, successfully bring down a moose. They eat their fill in about half an hour. Then they return home, and the pups nip at their snouts, begging for dinner. The adults immediately regurgitate undigested meat for the pups and babysitter to eat. Happy that a more appetizing meal is waiting for you on the plane, you slip away to begin your next adventure.

BY THE NUMBERS

1 litter of pups is born each year in a typical pack.

3 times bigger than a coyote, the gray wolf is the largest wild member of the dog family.

13 years is the average life span of a gray wolf in the wild.

22 pounds of meat may be wolfed down at one wolf's meal.

40 miles per hour is a wolf's top running speed.

100 times stronger sense of smell than a human's. A gray wolf can sense the presence of an animal up to three days after it's gone and smell prey more than a mile away.

Who's SMARTER ...
Cats or Dogs?

CATS FLUSH

Russ and Sandy Asbury were alone in their Whitewater, Wisconsin, home when they suddenly heard the toilet flush. "My husband's eyes got huge," says Sandy. "Did we have ghosts?"

Nope. Their cats just like to play with toilets. Boots, a Maine coon cat, taught himself to push on the handle that flushes. Then his copycat brother, Bandit, followed. "It's kind of eerie," Sandy admits. "Bandit follows me into the bathroom and flushes for me—sometimes even before I'm finished!"

Now the cats use the stunt to get attention. They go into a flushing frenzy if supper's late!

These cats just play in the bathroom, but some cats can be trained to use the toilet instead of a litter box. For their lucky owners, cleanup is just a flush (instead of a scoop) away. Meanwhile, Fido's just *drinking* from the toilet.

DOGS "GO" ON CUE

To housebreak a pup, take him outside and watch closely. When he starts to urinate, say the same phrase, such as "right there," each time. Within weeks, he'll associate the phrase with the action.

Buffy, a keeshond belonging to Wade Newman of Turin, New York, has never had an "accident" in the house. In fact, the smart dog sometimes plans ahead. Once, called in for the night, she came running. "But suddenly she stopped, cocked her head, and took off in the other direction," Newman says. "I was kind of annoyed." But it turned out Buffy was simply getting ready for bed—by "going" first, after which she obediently ran back to Newman. Now, *that's* thinking ahead!

DOGS SNIFF

Sometimes dogs can drive you crazy! That reportedly happened to one woman whose sheepdog started to sniff at her back every time she sat down. Exasperated, she asked her husband to take a look. All he saw was a dark mole. Nothing to worry about, thought the woman. Then one day she was sunbathing when her dog tried to nip off the mole with its teeth.

That did it. The woman went to the doctor and found out the mole was a deadly form of skin cancer. Her dog probably saved her life.

Dogs' noses have about 4 times as many scent cells as cats' noses and 14 times more than humans'. It makes some breeds terrific at sniffing out mold, termites, illegal drugs, missing persons, and, apparently, even cancer. Now, if only those noses didn't feel so cold.

CATS PREDICT EARTHQUAKES

Early one evening in 1976, people in northeastern Italy were all asking the same question: What is wrong with my cat? Many pets were running around, scratching on doors, and yowling to go out. Once out, they didn't come back (except for mother cats, who returned to get their kittens). Then, later that day, a major earthquake hit!

Cats may feel very early vibrations or sense the increase in static electricity that occurs before a quake. Whatever they're sensing, it's one more reason to pay attention to your cat.

DOGS PLAY THE PIANO

Forget "sit" and "shake." Chanda-Leah, a toy poodle who died in 2006 at the age of twelve, settled down at a computerized keyboard and plunked out "Twinkle, Twinkle, Little Star." Flashing red lights under the white keys told her which notes to hit.

"She loved to show off," says owner Sharon Robinson of Hamilton, Ontario, in Canada, who says the secret to training is practice and patience. That must be true, because Chanda knew a record-breaking number of tricks! She's the trickiest canine ever listed in *The Guinness Book of World Records*.

CATS WALK TIGHTROPES

Animal trainers of cats that appear in movies and TV commercials train the feline actors to walk on tightropes, wave at crowds, and open doors.

"Cats can do a lot, like jump through hoops, retrieve toys, and give high fives," says veterinarian Bonnie Beaver of Texas A&M University. But unlike dogs, they won't work for praise. "Cats are motivated by food," she says, "and it's got to be yummy."

So, which *is* smarter . . . a cat or a dog?

Actually, this is a trick question, and there's no simple answer.

Dogs and cats have different abilities. Each species knows what it needs to know in order to survive. "For that reason, we can't design a test that is equal for both animals," says Dr. Bonnie Beaver, a veterinarian at Texas A&M University. "When people ask me which is smarter, I say it's whichever one you own!"

TOP TEN MOST POPULAR DOG BREEDS	TOP TEN MOST POPULAR CAT BREEDS
1. LABRADOR RETRIEVER	1. PERSIAN
2. YORKSHIRE TERRIER	2. EXOTIC
3. GERMAN SHEPHERD	3. MAINE COON
4. GOLDEN RETRIEVER	4. SIAMESE
5. BEAGLE	5. ABYSSINIAN
6. BOXER	6. RAGDOLL
7. DACHSHUND	7. SPYHNX
8. BULLDOG	8. AMERICAN SHORTHAIR
9. POODLE	9. BIRMAN
10. SHIH TZU	10. ORIENTAL
(According to the American Kennel Club)	(According to the Cat Fanciers' Association)

Is there a "WOLF" in your house?

All dogs, from Chihuahuas to chow chows, are descended from wolves. So every dog is a little bit wolf. For thousands of years humans have bred dogs for the qualities that make them our best friends. Wolves are not dogs, however. They don't make good pets, and neither do wolf-dog crosses. Wolves are wild animals with predator instincts, and they can't be fully tamed.

5 COOL THINGS ABOUT ELEPHANTS

1 ELEPHANTS HAVE LONG MEMORIES

Elephants never forget. "They keep coming to places they like, no matter what," says photographer Frans Lanting, of Santa Cruz, California. One elephant herd has been visiting the same tree every November for at least 25 years!

2 ELEPHANTS CHAT WITH FRIENDS

Elephants are always "talking" in some way. This is fine in the wild. But it's a problem when elephants join sightseers on safari through the jungle. Noisy elephants spook wildlife away. "We depended on quiet," says John Roberts, who managed elephants at a lodge in the Royal Chitwan National Park in Nepal, in Asia.

When pachyderm pals Chan Chun Kali and Bhirikuti Kali worked together, they were too chatty, so Roberts moved the elephants to separate camps, six miles apart.

This worked during the day. But every night the chatterboxes started up again. They didn't rumble softly like most elephants do when "talking" long distance. "They shouted!" says Roberts. He wore earplugs to get some sleep.

3 ELEPHANTS THINK FOR THEMSELVES

In Thailand, the wild and wacky sport of elephant polo is popular. During one game, a player couldn't quite hit the ball—he just kept swinging and missing. Finally his quick-thinking elephant took matters into her own hands. She picked up the ball and handed it to the player!

4 ELEPHANTS ARE GENTLE

Tender touching is important among elephants. They hug, pet, and guide others with their trunks. Bob Norris, a cowboy from Colorado Springs, Colorado, adopted a baby African elephant named Amy. "We bonded immediately," he says.

5 ELEPHANTS HELP EACH OTHER

A retired circus elephant named Peggy might have drowned if another elephant hadn't come to her rescue! Peggy, an elephant with a partially paralyzed trunk, and her friend Betty Boop were bathing in the sanctuary pond, when Peggy laid down on her side. Swimming elephants use their trunks as snorkels, but Peggy's was completely underwater. The elephant couldn't breathe or stand! Luckily, Betty Boop rushed over and used her head to push Peggy back up on her feet and save her.

ELEPHANTS TO THE RESCUE

Trained elephants lent a helping "trunk" after a tsunami destroyed many of southern Asia's coastal towns in December 2004. In Thailand, the pachyderms used their trunks to lift motorcycles (right) and cars from the wreckage. Elephants also helped out in other countries hit by the tsunami. One elephant was walking with an eight-year-old girl on its back when the tsunami struck. In shoulder-high water, the elephant carried the girl to safety. Guess that makes these animals huge heroes!

SAFARI SEARCH

These young travelers have seen a lot of unusual African animals. The animal names in the box below are hidden in the safari jeep. They are horizontal, vertical, diagonal, even backward. When you spot them, circle them. **BONUS:** Find the animals in the picture!

aye-aye

flamingo

mamba

```
J E R B O A L L I R O G
N J E C H A M E L E O N X
X O Z E B R A A A S A O O T
K I M Q D H P M D I N K G O
A W D N A L E V V I E B D B E A N R
T N A I R A F A S Z N P A A I Y P I T
A B K H A I R Y F R O G B X E H I M O
E S K V N K R O T S U O B A R A M A I
T S E E B E D L I W O L Y R U N E L S
C H I C H I M P A N Z E E G R E T F E
P Q Y A S K          O G N O B F
     J P Q B          D V Z L
```

ibis

jerboa

bongo

wildebeest

Hidden Names

- aardvark
- addax
- ape
- baboon
- chameleon
- chimpanzee
- egret
- eland
- gorilla
- hairy frog
- hyena
- lion
- marabou stork
- okapi
- rhino
- safari ant
- skink
- tortoise
- zebra

The Weird World of FROGS

F rogs survived the catastrophic extinction of the dinosaurs. But strangely, the world's frogs and toads have suddenly begun to disappear. Some species that were common 25 years ago are now rare or extinct. And individual frogs are showing up with deformities such as too many legs. Scientists are not exactly sure what is going on.

But scientists do agree that because frogs drink and breathe through their thin skin, they are especially vulnerable to pesticides and pollution. A deformed frog often indicates that all is not well with the environment. And frogs live just about everywhere on Earth.

Frogs are amphibians, which means "double life." They generally hatch in water as tadpoles and end up living on land as fully formed frogs.

Frogs' skin must stay moist, so they're usually found in wet places.

Because frogs are so sensitive to environmental changes, they act as an early warning system. Their dwindling numbers may be a sign that our planet is not as clean and healthy as it once was. By studying how frogs are affected by the environment around them, scientists may be able to predict—and sound an alarm—that a neighborhood needs to cut back on lawn fertilizers or that a chemical-dumping factory should clean up its act. The hidden message in frogs' familiar peeps and croaks? "I'm jumpy for a reason!"

RANDOM Question

Q Has it ever rained frogs?

A Yes! Frogs fell from the sky in Kansas City, Missouri, in 1873, and again in De Witt, Arkansas, in 1942. Tornadoes and powerful storms sometimes vacuum up the surface of ponds, including the frogs living in the water. When the storm breaks up, frogs really *can* drop from the clouds!

CALLING ALL FROGS

Frogs bark, croak, cluck, click, grunt, snore, squawk, chirp, whistle, trill, and yap. Some are named for the noise they make. A chorus of barking tree frogs sounds like a pack of hounds on a hunt. The carpenter frog sounds like two carpenters hammering nails, and the pig frog grunts like—you guessed it—Porky's cousin! Here a male Australian red-eyed tree frog (above) inflates his throat pouch, which helps make his female-attracting calls louder.

TOADS and FROGS—WHICH IS WHICH?

Toads are actually a subgroup of the frog family. So scientifically speaking, all toads are frogs—but not all frogs are toads. Generally, the differences include the following:

AMERICAN TOAD   versus   BRONZE FROG

TOADS	FROGS
• have bumpy, dry skin	• have smooth, moist skin
• have short hind legs and move by short hops	• have long, strong hind legs and move by long leaps
• usually live in damp places, sometimes away from water	• often live in or near water, never found far from it

Superfrogs!

LARGEST
The Goliath frog, from West Africa, grows to about a foot long. As frogs grow, they shed their skins. After bending and twisting their bodies to loosen the skin, they pull it over their heads like a sweater—and eat it!

SMALLEST
One of the smallest frogs in the world, this leaf litter frog fits on a coin the size of a nickel. The tiny frog is found in Cuba. There are more than 4,500 species of frogs worldwide.

MOST POISONOUS
The bright colors of the golden poison-dart frog from Colombia, South America, warn predators to stay away. The skin of one golden poison-dart frog, the deadliest of all frog species, contains so much toxin it could kill 20,000 mice or 10 adult humans.

COOLEST
The North American wood frog spends two or three months frozen each winter. Its breathing and heartbeat stop, and most of the water in its body turns to ice. These frogs use a sugar called glucose in their blood as a kind of antifreeze to protect their organs from damage.

Frog Facts

Flashing open its big colorful eyes may help the red-eyed tree frog startle a predator just long enough for the frog to hop away.

The unusual gastric brooding frog of Australia is now probably extinct. But check this out: Mother frogs would swallow their eggs, and the young hatched in their stomachs. About six weeks later—burp!—up and out came fully formed froglets!

Some kinds of frogs lay as many as 30,000 eggs at a time.

Frogs can be different colors—green, brown, red, yellow, orange, and even blue!

Frogs have lived on Earth for so long—at least 190 million years—they were probably dodging dinosaurs!

WILD CAT
Family Reunion

There Are 37 Species of Wild Cats

Scientists divided them into eight groups called lineages after studying their DNA. Here are representatives from each lineage. The domestic house cat comes from the lineage that includes the sand cat.

1

CHEETAH
(46–143 pounds)
(21–65 kilograms)

• Often scans for prey from a high spot.

• Can sprint up to 70 miles an hour.

• From puma lineage, which includes three species.

2

CANADA LYNX
(11–38 pounds)
(5–15 kilograms)

• Its main prey is the snowshoe hare.

• Big paws act like snowshoes.

• From lynx lineage, which includes four species.

3

OCELOT
(15–34 pounds)
(6.8–15.4 kilograms)

• Most of an ocelot's prey is small.

• Found from Texas to Argentina.

• From ocelot lineage, which includes seven species.

4

TIGER
(165–716 pounds)
(74.8–324.8 kilograms)

• Tigers are the only striped wild cats.

• These big cats will hunt almost any mammal in their territory.

• From Panthera lineage, which includes seven species, such as lion and jaguar.

AND CAT (3–7.5 pounds) (1.4–3.4 kilograms)
The sand cat lives in dry deserts of northern Africa and the Middle East.

Rarely drinks; gets water from food.

From domestic cat lineage, which includes six species of cat.

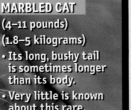

MARBLED CAT
(4–11 pounds)
(1.8–5 kilograms)

- Its long, bushy tail is sometimes longer than its body.
- Very little is known about this rare, nocturnal, and shy wild cat.
- From bay cat lineage, which includes three species.

6

SERVAL
(15–30 pounds)
(6.8–13.6 kilograms)

7

- Longest legs, relative to its body, of any cat species.
- Big ears used to listen for prey.
- From caracal lineage, which includes three species.

8

FISHING CAT
(11–35 pounds)
(5–15.8 kilograms)

- A strong swimmer, it has slightly webbed feet.
- Eats mainly fish.
- From leopard cat lineage, which includes five species.

How to tell a cat by its SPOTS

JAGUAR: little dots in the middle of larger rings
Home: mainly Mexico, Central and South America
Average Size: 80 to 350 pounds
Cat Fact: Third-largest in the cat family after tigers and lions, the jaguar is the largest feline in the Western Hemisphere.

LEOPARD: rings without the jaguar's smaller dots inside
Home: much of Asia and Africa
Average Size: 62 to 200 pounds
Cat Fact: Some leopards are dark and look spotless. They're called black panthers.

CHEETAH: evenly spaced, solid black splotches the size of a human thumbprint
Home: parts of Africa
Average Size: 46 to 143 pounds
Cat Fact: Fastest land animal; dark lines mark a cheetah's face from the inner corner of each eye to the outer corners of its mouth.

SERVAL: usually a series of single black dots that can vary from the size of a freckle to that of a quarter
Home: many parts of Africa
Average Size: 15 to 30 pounds
Cat Fact: A serval uses its huge ears to hunt by sound, surprising prey with a pounce.

OCELOT: solid or open-centered dark spots that sometimes merge to look like links in a chain; fur in the center of open spots is often darker than background coat color
Home: South, Central, and North America
Average Size: 15 to 34 pounds
Cat Fact: An ocelot's main prey is rodents.

GREAT WHITE SHARKS

You Are Here

CONTINENT AND COUNTRY: AUSTRALIA

LOCATION: SPENCER GULF OFF THE COAST OF SOUTH AUSTRALIA

UNIQUE: ONLY COUNTRY THAT IS ALSO A CONTINENT

"We've located a great white shark," the captain tells you and the shark expert you've been talking with on the deck of the research vessel. You're off the coast of South Australia, near Spencer Gulf. The captain points to the shark cage tied to the boat's stern. "Hop in!" he tells you. "This is an opportunity you won't want to miss."

You check your snorkeling gear and then slip down feetfirst into the cage. (A shark cage is built to keep great white sharks out. The cage's metal bars protect divers like you.) Slowly you're lowered, inside the cage, to just below the ocean surface. Soon you spot what you came to see. Your heart races as a six-foot great white shark glides past the cage, turns, and swims by again. You are safe.

Great white sharks are the world's largest meat-eating fish. Their sharp teeth and powerful jaws are built to cut and tear their prey. The longest confirmed great white was longer than 20 feet—about the length of 4 bathtubs! Your six-footer is a young shark.

Suddenly you see the shark's impressive teeth. The predator you're watching speeds by again—this time following a school of large fish. The shark grabs one that lags a bit behind the rest. In two gulps, the fish is gone. The scientist on board told you that great white sharks also scavenge, or eat dead animals they come across. They particularly like whales. Whale blubber, or fat, gives these large sharks an excellent source of calories. Now the captain hoists you out of the water because the time has come to head for dry land.

Steering Clear of Shark Bites

Shark attacks on people are extremely rare. In the U.S., seven times as many people are bitten by squirrels as sharks every year. Here are tips to help you stay safe:

1 Stay out of the ocean at dawn, dusk, and night—when some sharks swim into shallow water to feed.

2 Don't swim in the ocean if you're bleeding.

3 Swim and surf at beaches with lifeguards on duty. They can warn you about shark sightings.

6 COOL THINGS YOU DIDN'T KNOW ABOUT SHARKS

1 TEETH TO SPARE

If great white sharks had tooth fairies, they'd be rich! A great white loses and replaces thousands of its teeth during its lifetime. Its upper jaw is lined with 26 front-row teeth; its lower jaw has 24. Behind these razor-sharp points are many rows of replacement teeth. The "spares" move to the front whenever the shark loses a tooth.

2 BOX OFFICE BULLY

Great white sharks are superstars. Before the *Star Wars* series, the 1975 movie *Jaws* was Hollywood's biggest moneymaker. *Jaws*, about a great white on the prowl, cost $12 million to film but made $260 million in the U.S. Not bad for a fish story!

3 SPEEDY SWIMMERS

Great white sharks can sprint through the water at speeds of 35 miles per hour—seven times faster than the best Olympic swimmer! Scientists on the California coast tracked one shark as it swam all the way to Hawaii—2,400 miles—in only 40 days.

4 CHOW DOWN, TUNA BREATH!

Picky eaters they're not. While great white sharks prefer to eat seals, sea lions, and the occasional dolphin, they've been known to swallow lots of other things. Bottles, tin cans, a straw hat, lobster traps, and a cuckoo clock are among the items found inside the bellies of great white sharks.

5 EAR THAT?

Great white sharks have ears. You can't see them, because they don't open to the outside. The sharks use two small sensors in the skull to hear and, perhaps, to zero in on the splashing sounds of a wounded fish or a struggling seal!

6 HOT ON THE TRAIL

Unlike most fish, great white sharks' bodies are warmer than their surroundings. The sharks' bodies can be as much as 27°F (-3°C) warmer than the water the fish swim in. A higher temperature helps the great white shark swim faster and digest its food more efficiently—very useful for an animal that's always on the go!

Sensitive Sharks

What's the secret weapon a great white shark or a black-tip reef shark uses to track its prey? Gel in the snout! The clear gel acts like a highly sensitive thermometer, registering changes in water temperature as slight as a thousandth of a degree, according to a University of San Francisco physicist. Tiny changes in the ocean's temperature tend to occur in places where cold and warm water mix, feeding areas for smaller fish—a shark's next meal. Once the gel registers a change, it produces an electrical charge that causes nerves in the snout to send a message to the shark's brain that says, "Let's do lunch!"

BY THE NUMBERS

ABOUT **12** species of sharks are considered dangerous.

YOU ARE **250** times more likely to be killed by lightning than by a shark.

THERE ARE **375** different species of sharks found in the world's oceans.

THERE WERE **43,674** more injuries associated with toilets than with sharks.

MEET THE NAT GEO EXPLORER

SYLVIA EARLE

Sometimes termed "Her Deepness," Earle is an oceanographer, explorer, author, and lecturer, whose knowledge of the sea is immense. Earle has led more than 60 expeditions and logged more than 6,000 hours underwater, including leading the first team of women aquanauts during the Tektite Project in 1970 and setting a record for solo diving to a depth of 3,300 feet (1,000 meters).

How did you become an explorer?
It was really easy. I started out as a kid, asking questions—Who? How? What? Where? When? And especially, why? And I never stopped. Explorers and scientists never lose their sense of wonder, never stop asking questions, and always keep looking for answers.

What was your closest call in the field?
I have been surrounded by hundreds of sharks, dived in submersibles more than two miles under the sea, and had my air supply run out when I was more than a thousand feet away from my home base underwater.

How did you get involved with National Geographic?
I loved reading the *NATIONAL GEOGRAPHIC* magazine as a child, and I still do. Then, as a scientist, I lived underwater for two weeks in 1970, and I was asked to write about the experience for *NATIONAL GEOGRAPHIC!* Since then I have written more stories for the magazine and worked on a lot of films and books.

Would you suggest that kids follow in your footsteps?
I followed my heart—and it led into the sea. I hope every child will have a chance to realize his or her dreams. Every person has a special, unique pathway that unfolds as opportunities arise and choices are made. There is an urgent need for everyone who cares about exploring and protecting natural systems, above and below the sea, to get busy and go for it!

EMPEROR PENGUINS

1 Emperors are the largest of the 17 penguin species.

2 One colony can number as many as 60,000 penguins.

3 These penguins can live 20 years or more in the wild.

4 Emperors eat fish, squid, and shrimplike krill.

5 Parents feed chicks every three to four days.

GO FISH!

Something's fishy at this aquarium. Find and circle the following items that are hidden in this scene.

- **surfboard**
- **cowboy hat**
- **sunflower**
- **wrapped gift**
- **bike wheel**
- **teacup and saucer**
- **plate of spaghetti**
- **soft pretzel**
- **guitar**

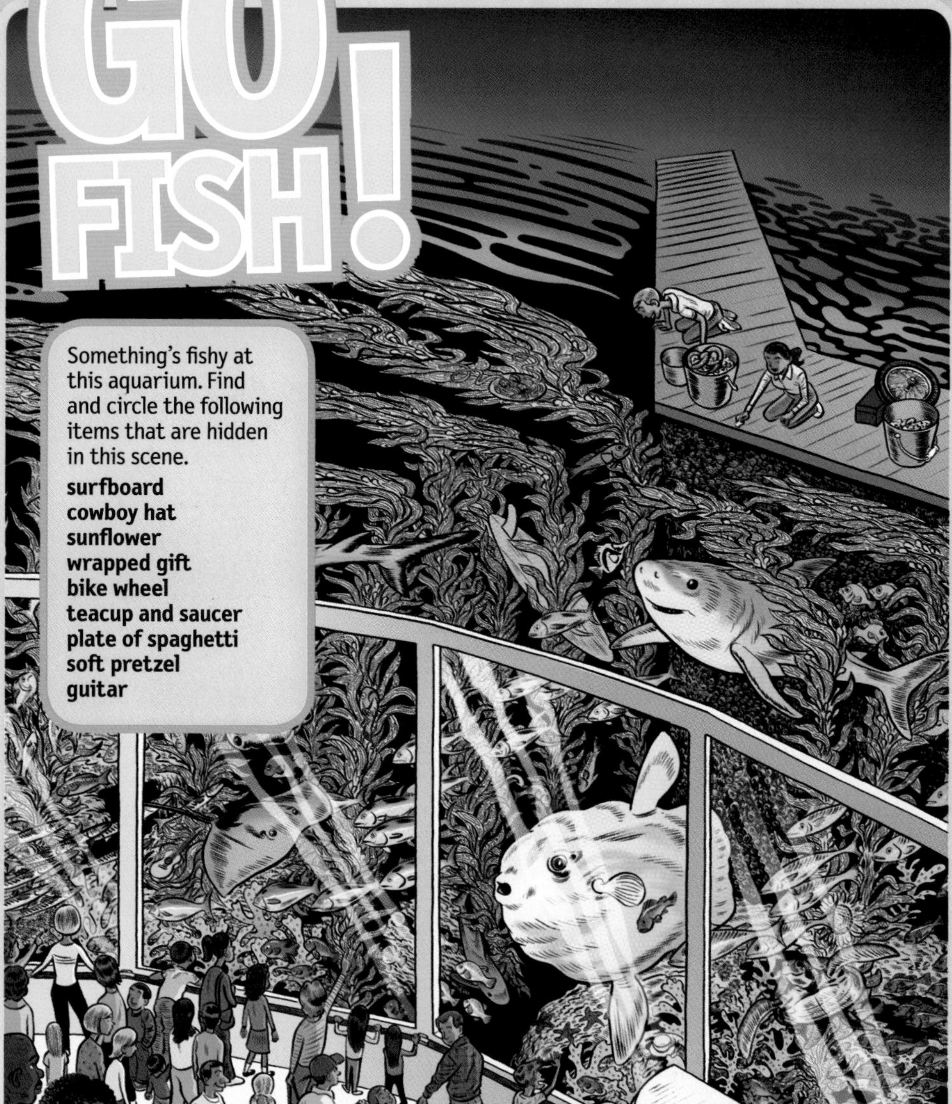

PANDAMONIUM

Like a toddler at snack time, a giant panda sits with its legs stretched out in front of it and munches on bamboo. The tough bamboo is no match for the panda's powerful jaws and the crushing force of its huge molars. In one day, it'll polish off 20 to 40 pounds of bamboo!

Bamboo—a grass that grows tall like a tree—sprouts so fast you can actually watch it grow. Even so, nearly 138 giant pandas starved to death in the mid-1970s.

Today, there are fewer than 2,500 pandas left in the wild. Another loss would devastate the endangered population.

BLOOMING BAMBOO

For pandas, bamboo is the perfect food and shelter. Ninety-nine percent of a panda's diet is bamboo. Stems, shoots, leaves—pandas devour it all. That is, until the bamboo begins to flower. Even the hungriest panda isn't likely to eat it at that stage, because bamboo is not nutritious or appetizing as it flowers.

One blooming plant wouldn't be a big deal, but bamboo is peculiar. Unlike most plants, when one bamboo flowers, all of the bamboo plants of the same species do, too. After flowering, bamboo drops its seeds to the forest floor. Then the plant dies. If a majority of a forest is the same species of bamboo, then pandas are suddenly out of food.

FINDING FOOD

You would think that a panda would be able to hunker down and wait out the flowering by surviving on other plants and small animals. But many species of bamboo sprouts aren't big enough to be edible for at least five to seven years. That means a small area—or an entire forest—goes from a bamboo buffet to starvation central practically overnight—and stays that way.

Scientists know very little about the bamboo flowering process because it happens so infrequently. Some haven't flowered in 120 years—when your great-grandparents or maybe even great-great-grandparents were still in diapers.

In the past, pandas would just search for other sources of bamboo. Today there's a short supply of dining digs because roads, farms, cities, logging, and mining isolate forests. The pandas can't get to a suitable new forest because their homes are surrounded by human activities.

LOOKING AHEAD

To halt habitat destruction, China has stopped most logging. The government also created some 50 nature reserves for pandas. And scientists are working with zoos worldwide to create an extensive panda breeding program with a goal of rebuilding the wild population. All this support gives giant pandas—and their bamboo habitat—a green future.

Where Bears Live

Bear Ranges
- American Black Bear
- Asiatic Black Bear
- Brown Bear
- Giant Panda
- Polar Bear
- Sloth Bear
- Spectacled Bear
- Sun Bear

Striped pattern indicates overlapping ranges.

0 —— 3,000 miles
0 —— 4,000 kilometers

BROWN BEARS

📷 CLOSE-UP

Look, Ma. No Hands!

Open wide! Fish—it's what's for dinner. This salmon did not look before it leaped, so it's about to end up as brown bear food. Salmon by the thousands leave the ocean and head upstream to mate and lay eggs every fall. Attracted by the fish feast, brown bears by the dozen gather along the banks of Brooks Falls in Katmai National Park in Alaska to fatten up before their long winter hibernation. Timing, luck, and patience are what helped photographer Joel Sartore catch this fish—just before the bear did.

Q Are GUINEA PIGS really related to PIGS?

A No. Guinea pigs are actually the cuter cousins of rats and other rodents. But their stocky bodies and high-pitched squeals make them look and sound like miniature porkers. Naturally when Europeans first saw these South American fur balls in the 1500s, they named the rodents after their farm animal look-alikes. So why are they called "guinea" pigs? No one knows for sure. One theory is that the animals once cost a guinea, an old English coin. Guinea pigs may be misnamed, but at least they don't have to live in a pigsty!

"Um . . . my owner ate my homework."

Why should cats and dogs get all the attention? Here's what makes other pets so special. See if one of them is right for you.

HORSE

If you have the time and money for a horse, pick one for its behavior, not its breed.

GOLDFISH

Too busy? Goldfish won't chew up your shoes if you come home late.

PARAKEET

Parakeets can be trained to talk and will perch on your finger.

Pampered PET

Today's celebrities may dress up their dogs in silly designer clothes and doggie jewelry, but that's nothing new. People have been spoiling their four-legged and feathered friends for thousands of years.

Pampering your pet could cost you an arm and a paw!

LUXURY SUITE AT PET SPA	**$75** A NIGHT
PROFESSIONAL MASSAGE	**$30**
CUSTOM-BUILT DOGHOUSE	**$6,000**
CUSTOM-MADE PET SOFA	**$400**
HAND-KNITTED SWEATER	**$250**
GOURMET DOG TREATS	**$5** FOR 13 OUNCES

In the 1800s, Hai Lung, a long-haired Pekingese, had his own servant and snoozed in a basket lined with red silk. The royal pup couldn't even chow down on his chopped liver until the food had been inspected by his owner—the ruler of China!

Dog Bed

Try This!

WHAT YOU'LL NEED

- **FLEECE FABRIC IN TWO COLORS (AVAILABLE AT FABRIC STORES); THE AMOUNT OF FABRIC DEPENDS ON THE SIZE OF YOUR DOG.**
- **RULER**
- **FABRIC SCISSORS**
- **POLYESTER PILLOW STUFFING**
- **OPTIONAL: OTHER COLORS OF FLEECE TO DECORATE THE PILLOW**

WHAT TO DO

Determine the dimensions your pillow needs to be to fit your dog; then add eight inches to the length and width. (This gives you extra fabric for fringe.) Measure two colors of fleece to this size and align both pieces. To create the fringe, cut strips four inches long by one inch wide along all four sides of both pieces of fleece. Cut out the squares of fabric at the corners. (If you like, cut extra fabric into fun shapes and sew them onto the fleece that will form the pillow's top.) Tightly knot the top strips to the bottom strips on three sides of the pillow. Stuff the pillow filling into the open side until the pillow is firm. Then tie the last side together.

AYE-AYES OF MADAGASCAR

The aye-aye's odd-looking fingers, pointy teeth, big eyes, and huge ears give some people the creeps.

Seeing an aye-aye is considered very bad luck to many superstitious residents of Madagascar, the African island country where these animals live in the wild. In parts of the country, people kill aye-ayes on sight, hoping to prevent anything "evil" from happening. The aye-aye's bad reputation isn't helped by the fact that it's active only at night, when things can seem a lot scarier to people.

The truth about this five-pound animal, a type of lemur, is that it's harmless. In the wild, aye-ayes live mostly in trees. When they leave their nests, where they spend daylight hours sleeping, their forest home is dark. Big eyes help them see as they look for food. Aye-ayes' favorite food is insect larvae.

The main threat to aye-ayes is loss of habitat due to farming and logging in Madagascar. Added to that danger are the people who kill them because of lingering beliefs that aye-ayes bring bad luck. We can only hope that fears about the animals will disappear at the same time aye-ayes' numbers grow.

AFRICA

MADAGASCAR

MADAGASCAR

■ AREAS WHERE AYE-AYES MAY LIVE

ANIMAL KILLERS

BUSTED!

GUNNING FOR TROUBLE

The bald eagle bodies arrived at the lab by the dozens, shot, with their tails and wings missing. No gun had been heard, and no hunter was sighted where police had discovered the corpses.

But the killer left key evidence. The casings, or outer shells, of his bullets littered the ground beneath the telephone wires where he'd shot the protected national birds.

A gun leaves telltale nicks and scratches on the bullets it fires. "We can match both the bullets and the casings to a particular weapon by the marks left on them after they've been fired from the gun," says deputy lab director Ed Espinoza.

Back in the lab, the forensic scientists recovered the bullets that killed several eagles. Then they fired a test round of bullets from a gun seized from a suspect.

Using a high-powered microscope, investigators compared scratches from the test round to scratches on bullets found in the eagles. They matched perfectly. Thanks to the scientists' eagle eyes, the suspect was charged. Bald eagles are now safe from this bad guy.

CRIME SCENE EVIDENCE

BULLET

CRIME SCENE EVIDENCE

FEATHER SAMPLE

ULTIMATE Animal RESCUE

Molly can relax in her new home.

Molly, an African lioness, was found prowling in a Dallas, Texas, neighborhood. She was starving, and a chain around her neck was choking her. Rescuers cut it off with bolt cutters and hurried her to a veterinarian. Fortunately a good permanent home awaited the ten-month-old abandoned pet as she began her journey back to health.

Located in Austin, Texas, the 20-acre Austin Zoo is a private, nonprofit organization that takes in and rehabilitates all sorts of confiscated, stray, or unwanted animals. The zoo staff never tries to make them act like pets. Like most zoos, it's open to the public, but the Austin Zoo does not breed or sell any of its animals. It even becomes home for animals that other zoos no longer want to keep.

Now Nikki has room to climb.

In her new home, Molly eats a proper diet, and she has gained weight. She lives there with other abandoned pets like Nikki, a ring-tailed lemur, and Teri, a Brazilian porcupine. Both Nikki and Teri like to climb around branches and platforms.

Nearby, Binny the bearcat lounges on his little house

or slowly stretches out on the tree branches in his large, private enclosure. That's a whole lot better than napping on someone's doorstep after escaping from the barn where he was kept illegally. Although he is called a bearcat, Binny isn't related to either bears or cats. *Bearcat* is another name for binturong, an animal species from Asia.

Teri the porcupine

The Austin Zoo gets nearly 200 calls a month about animals

in need of homes, but unfortunately they don't have room for all of them. The solution for neglected exotic pets, zoos' unwanted animals, and animals rescued from bad conditions isn't building more animal sanctuaries. It's important to stop breeding these animals instead. But for the lucky animals the zoo has helped to save, now numbering more than 300 individuals of more than 100 different species, the Austin Zoo is one home sweet home.

A worker makes sure Binny is OK.

Gorilla RESCUE

Orphaned and afraid, baby gorilla Dunia finally finds kindness in human arms.

When a terrified one-year-old baby gorilla was found in a sting operation against poachers (illegal hunters) in Rwanda, the authorities rushed the young gorilla to the nearby head-quarters of the Mountain Gorilla Veterinary Project. The vets there realized that she had not been given enough food or water, but they were more worried about something else she hadn't been getting: touch. Surprisingly, gorillas, animals well known for their great size and strength, are extremely fragile creatures—they need their mother's constant body contact to survive. The project's staff immediately began holding and cuddling the little female—a kind of touch first aid. They named her Dunia. After six months of loving care that included around-the-clock attention, a good diet, and a comfortable home at the project's headquarters, Dunia was looking and acting like a healthy, happy young gorilla should. Eventually, the vets at the project hope to place Dunia and other orphaned gorillas in a sanctuary. No matter where she ends up, Dunia will never be alone again.

How you can help!

Be careful with the products you buy. Don't buy or sell products from dead wildlife, such as ivory from elephants. Live cruelty-free.

Reach out to animal rights groups to help make life better for wild animals and help protect their rights.

Read all you can about animals and the issues surrounding them. Knowledge is power.

Cougar RESCUE

Chinook and another orphaned cougar cub snuggle at the Oregon Zoo.

When a scared and hungry orphaned cougar cub wandered into a neighborhood searching for food, the homeowners called the au-thorities for help. This cub was starving. She weighed only 20 pounds, half what she should have weighed. "She probably would have died in a matter of days," says state fish and wildlife officer Larry Baker. Cougars normally stay with their mothers until they're about two years old, nursing and then learning how to catch prey.

The cub needed medical attention right away. In addition to starva-tion, the cougar suffered from fleas and internal parasites. With the help of medicine and meaty meals, the cat quickly gained weight and strength. But she could not be released into the wild without the survival skills her mother would have taught her. After three months of recovery, Chinook, as she was named, was taken to a new, permanent home at the Oregon Zoo in Portland.

There, the zoo's staff keeps her busy and exercised. She "hunts" for meals and gets frozen meat treats. What does Chinook like to do the most? Sleep, like most cougars.

Saving Habitats

A habitat is a place where animals and plants live. Animals adapt to their specific habitats—forest, desert, ocean, prairie, wherever—to find food, hide from predators, and raise young. But if one thing changes, the habitat could be in trouble.

For instance, building houses and shopping malls can change or even destroy habitats. And constructing roads can divide habitats, creating barriers to food and shelter. Such changes make it hard for animals to survive.

Think of it this way: What if your refrigerator stopped working, or your faucets ran dry? One small change could make your house—your habitat—unlivable. And just like you, animals and plants need safe, livable habitats to survive.

Don Edwards San Francisco Bay National Wildlife Refuge (NWR*)
California
In this urban habitat, American avocets hunt on mudflats, which can contain 40,000 living things in a handful of mud.

Agassiz NWR
Minnesota
This refuge supports the largest population of gray wolves in the lower 48 states.

Horicon NWR
Wisconsin
Migrating birds such as redhead ducks nest at this freshwater refuge.

John Heinz NWR at Tinicum
Pennsylvania
Like many wildlife refuges, this NWR is within an hour's drive of a major U.S. city.

National Bison Range
Montana
American bison grow thick fur for the chilly winters here.

Rocky Mountain Arsenal NWR
Colorado
Bald eagles spread their wings over this prairie habitat, an inactive military site.

Canaan Valley NWR
West Virginia
Black bears roam in the swamps and forests of this refuge, the system's 500th.

Cabeza Prieta NWR
Arizona
Saguaro cactuses living here survive deserts by storing as much as seven tons of water.

Wichita Mountains NWR
Oklahoma
Prairie dogs dig burrows that become habitats for many grassland creatures.

Neal Smith NWR
Iowa
The regal fritillary butterfly is getting a helping hand from this refuge's 8,600-acre prairie restoration project.

Okefenokee NWR
Georgia
Although the American alligator is thriving, many of its unprotected wetland habitats are shrinking.

Pelican Island NWR
Florida
Protected at the first National Wildlife Refuge, brown pelicans live only near coasts.

Kenai NWR
Alaska
Salmon thrive in this watershed, a source of water for rivers and streams.

Kilauea Point NWR
Hawai'i
Laysan albatross chicks face little threat from predators on this coastal refuge.

*National Wildlife Refuges (NWRs) are home to hundreds of species of birds, mammals, reptiles, fish, and plants, including endangered species. The U.S. Fish and Wildlife Service manages more than 540 refuges. Check out a few of them on this map, or go online to learn more—including how to visit one! www.fws.gov/refuges

23

ANIMALS THAT YOU MIGHT RUN INTO AT SCHOOL

HMMM — BOOKWORM

I SAW THAT! — BALD EAGLE

PSST! SHOW ME YOUR ANSWERS. — THE CHEETAH

I KNOW WHO DID IT. — A RAT

CREATE YOUR OWN HYBRID ANIMAL.

Try This!

DRAW A PICTURE THAT IS A COMBINATION OF TWO ANIMALS.

GROUPIES!

Fish swim in schools, and cattle hang out in herds, but check out these weird names for other animal groups:

- a cloud of grasshoppers
- a sloth of bears
- a business of ferrets
- a troop of monkeys
- a plague of locusts
- a bloat of hippos
- an army of caterpillars
- a crash of rhinos

- a stand of flamingos
- a murder of crows
- a gaggle of geese
- a string of ponies
- a skulk of foxes
- an ostentation of peacocks
- a knot of toads
- a trip of goats

- a rafter of turkeys
- a peep of chickens
- a husk of hares
- a paddling of ducks
- a bale of turtles
- a pod of whales
- a drift of hogs
- a smack of jellyfish

Printed in U.S.A.
16/KG/6